I0170994

Matome Liphy Ramalepe

Praising with an upright heart

MATOME LIPHY RAMALEPE

PRAISING WITH AN UPRIGHT HEART

REARABILWE AFRICA SOLUTIONS PTY LTD
Publishing, Leadership and Research Solutions

Copyright © 2016 by Matome L Ramalepe

All rights reserved

Written permission must be secured from the publisher to use or reproduce any part of this book, except for brief quotations in critical reviews or article.

ISBN: 978-0-620-70085-6

Published by:

Rearabilwe Africa Solutions Pty Ltd

P O Box 2314

Tzaneen

0850

www.rearabilweafricasolutions.co.za

Dedications

"To the Source and Sustainer of life and all true gifts, may your truth contained in this book explode in the hearts of all who read it. To my beloved wife, Sarah, and my children, Haraepha, Horeloketsi and Rearabilwe, thank you for your support, patience and cooperation while I pursue the many projects included in my earthly assignments. You are all my pearls. To all the members of our church 'Kingdom of Priests Assembly International', thanks for dreaming with me and teaching me how to lead and follow.

"What a fascinating piece of work! It makes me to repent and repent all over again because of the truth it unfolds to me as a worshiper. I can say with no doubt that my worship style and attitude will never be the same again. Certainly, this finer resource will help every worshipper who encounters it to form a heart of praise."

Mrs. Malatji Sithembile Sizakele
Worship Leader
(Church on the Rock)

"I feel so blessed to have been present when Dr Ramalepe preached the message 'mbilu ya munhu yi borile' 'a man's heart is deceitful' at Gabaza. This makes me relate closely with the section entitled 'The Gabaza Experience' and I feel everyone who was present when the message was delivered should read it. This section clearly reveals the underlying point of the book that the Master Planner's will through praise is realised through a repentant heart of service, humility and submission."

Pastor Chabalala Charity Morris

New Everlasting Covenant Ministries

Contents

Foreword

Aglance through the pages of this book will show that it is a concise and informative book full of quality material. It is laden with gems of revelations. I am totally unaware of any book that had treated the subject of praise and worship from this angle before. I am thrilled to see how the book articulates and reflects our church's motto "Holiness precedes sacrifices." Dr Apostle Ramalepe coined the motto in 2010 as a means by which he sought to communicate his belief that a worshipper's character matters more than the worshipper's sacrifices and services. Therefore, this book challenges Christians to seek to express praise from an upright heart and offer themselves as acceptable sacrifices before God. It clearly unveils that the nature of the worship service is not determined by the elaborate sets of instruments, but by the attributes of those who play them. If followed, the principles expounded here will keep any congregation fresh and progressive in its praise and worship. It will guide pastors and worship leaders on what to consider when appointing worshippers to serve in their church worship teams.

Pastor Peter Mahasha

(Kingdom of Priests Assembly International)

January 2016

The 'Gabaza' Experience

"What comes from the inside defiles the outside

After three years of writing this book, I regret that I did not encounter this experience sooner. Most of what I wrote about in this book could have been thoroughly refined. Nevertheless, the valuable lessons I take from this experience are a 'makeover' for this book, making it the finest resource for pastors and worship leaders who are serious about igniting their praise and worship ministries. Halfway through the proofreading of the last two chapters of this book, I was requested to preach in a memorial service of one of our colleague's mother in law in a village called Gabaza. Gabaza is a predominantly Tsonga speaking village situated furthest away from the town of Tzaneen in Mopani District, Limpopo Province. Despite the enemy's use of some scare tactics to unsettle me with stories of witchcraft in the area, I still encountered a significant learning experience that helped me to reconceptulise the upright heart as the heart of praise.

On the day of the memorial, I arrived after people have already converged in the tent, singing hymns, waiting for the programme director of the day to get the service underway. I could not immediately sit in the tent because I sensed a heavy presence of the satanic forces sent to counter the preaching of God's word.

It was only then that I vividly recollected the witchcraft stories I was told before. I became edgy at once and thought to myself, if I had not been sceptical about these stories, maybe I would have interceded for the village more. Suddenly, I felt a pressing need in my spirit to intercede for the teachers and villagers in the tent. I went straight to the rest room (lavatory), rebuked the enemy, and sought God's divine intervention through the spoken word. When it was a time to give the sermon, I wrestled with demonic oppression for a while; nevertheless, I received a breakthrough after I sung a praise hymn. Then, the Holy Spirit led me to preach under a Tsonga title, 'Mbilo yi borile', which means 'The heart is deceitful and extremely sick.' The title was drawn from Jeremiah 17:9. Not only was the message spiritually enlightening and delivering, but it also generated several constructive comments from both the villagers and the teachers afterwards. The message also earned me a nickname 'A heart Pastor' from the villagers who insisted I should return to the village and start a church.

The lessons I received from the comments make this message stand out from the messages I ever preached at memorial services. After reflection, I boiled everything down to four perspectives. These four perspectives now form the basis for understanding the nature and influence of an upright heart as articulated in the five chapters of the book. I have focused on these four perspectives because they serve as a grid for how I interpret contemporary praise and worship, determine what a true worshipper looks like, and guide the decisions I take in selecting worship leaders in our church.

A man's heart determines and shapes a man's actions and words.

In their native languages, both the people of Gabaza and the teachers pointed out that people say what they say and act the way they act influenced by their own hearts. Action and word are the two aspects involved in praise. Praise is simply an expression of approval and admiration, to applaud, to extol, to magnify and glorify. Praise is expressed through actions and words – through singing, shouting, speaking forth, dancing, and playing musical instruments. I am therefore correct to say that nothing affects how we act and what we say during praise more than our hearts. Regarding words we utter in praise, our Lord Jesus Christ states that "Out of the abundance of the heart the mouth speaks" (Matthew 12:34d). About our actions in praise and worship, the story of Saul in 1 Samuel 13:6-14 teaches us that whatever is in a man's heart determines a man's actions.

When arrogance entered Saul's heart, he took things into his own hands and sacrificed the burnt offerings. Samuel calls his action "a foolish thing to do." He called this act 'foolish' because only priests were allowed to sacrifice offerings, but Saul trespassed on this rule. In so doing, Saul miserably failed a test for fitness to hold office as a leader of Israel. Saul's downfall came about by his failure to guard his own heart. Solomon's wise instruction is valid, "Above all else, guard your heart, for it is the wellspring of life" (Proverbs 4:23, NIV). When arrogance and rebellion enter a man's heart, a man acts imprudently and speaks unwisely. A man can only bring forth good or evil actions and words out of the treasure of his heart.

Only God searches and tests the heart and examines its secret motives.

Unless otherwise spiritually gifted in prophecy or discernment, no person is capable of knowing what is in the heart of another. Only God examines the secret motives of our hearts to give us our due rewards. When you have bought a brand new car and two people approach you, both of them say the same words of congratulations, you do not know whose words are sincere. One of them might be saying one thing with the mouth and another with the heart. You may not be hearing the voice of his or her heart, but God hears it clearly. He will certainly judge according to the words of the heart rather than the words of the mouth.

What comes from the inside defiles the outside.

It is what comes from our hearts that pollutes our marriages, institutions and governments. Evil seen in the outside world is evil in the inside world. Before rape and murder are committed 'out' there, it is rape and murder committed 'in' here (heart). Therefore, to deal with these criminal practices we need to deal with the heart first. Campaigns against violence, though necessary, cannot have immediate impact if the hearts of men are drenched with violence. Getting rid of violence in the heart is getting rid of violence in homes and workplaces. Our Lord Jesus said to his disciples, 'Whatever comes from [the heart of] man that is what defiles and dishonors him". We note a list of things that come from within that corrupt a man and his world: the acts of greed and covetousness, acts of sexual immorality, theft, murders, adulteries, arrogance, envy and jealous, self-righteousness, malevolent thoughts, foolishness [poor judgment] (Mark 7:21, 22 AMP]. All these vile things are vomits from the heart, and they defile the world we live in. The source of the world's pollution is what comes out of the heart of people dwelling in it. To change the world will, therefore, require that we try to change the hearts of people living in the world.

In July 2015, I read an interesting online article by Stephen Grootes published in the Daily Maverick entitled "South Africa: Would things be different without Zuma?" In his article, Stephen asks two interesting questions, "If Zuma were not president, what would the situation look like?" and "Would any of our fundamental problems really be solved?" He then asserted that the corruption is completely intertwined with President Zuma personally. Considering his many scandals, and of course, twin disasters of his relationship with the Guptas and Nkandla itself, Stephen likened Zuma to a Metro cop who demands a cool drink. His argument was simply that Zuma has certainly come to symbolise a major problem in South Africa, with the example he sets having a corrosive effect on people in other government institutions. If the comments that followed Stephen's article is anything to go by, it seems many people believe South Africa would be better without Jacob Zuma.

To add salt to already septic wound, President Zuma irrationally, recklessly and unceremoniously axed the former finance minister Ndladla Nene in December 2015. This move plummeted the South African economy into crisis. The Rand collapsed, and in the wake of this Rand fiasco, a great uproar ensued in the country. Many South Africa citizens were baying for the president's blood. They believed that South Africa would be a better place without Jacob Zuma as Number one. Almost all the opposition parties called for the president's immediate resignation. After reading many articles, I found myself strongly sharing the sentiments of many South Africans that Zuma's corruption and lack of effective governing skills had had profoundly negative effects on the country. I also believed that there are of course, areas where the situation would be very different without Zuma at the helm of the country.

However, I think it is a mistake to think that much of this would change if we change the president. Now the question is, "If changing the President won't solve our entire crisis, what is an alternative solution?" While contemplating on an immediate solution, a crazy idea bounced into my mind. I remembered what I once said, "A visible change in the outside could only come as a result of a change in the inside." A permanent solution should therefore be to try to change the president's heart rather than to dismiss him. Perhaps, the important question is, "How are we going to do it?" Take him to Constitutional Court? A resounding, no! No court in the land can succeed in changing a man's heart. One instrument I do know that has unassailable power to change people's hearts is God's Word. I am fully aware of the fact that the change of heart can only take effect as soon as a person receives God's spoken word. So, if the president cannot receive God's word, there is no way we can change his heart. And if his heart cannot be changed, his actions cannot change either. For what comes from the inside corrupts the outside.

Let me admit, though, that this solution is too weird to share on social media. It seems impractical and too spiritual, and it would seem undependable during this time when the country needs urgent interventions. But my argument is that what the president does out there is because of what he has harboured in there [in his heart]. Therefore, crisis in South Africa does not require political solution. It requires spiritual solution. To realise spiritual intervention we need to use God's spiritual scalpel to cut through into the hearts of our president and his cabinet ministers.

God chooses the heart, not the man.

When Saul did something foolish God's prophet and priest announced his judgment, "But now your kingdom will not endure, the Lord has sought out a man after his own heart and appointed him leader of his people, because you have not kept the Lord's command" (1 Sam 13:14, NIV). When Saul's heart became arrogant and treated with contempt the living God, the living God left heaven and searched the earth for his replacement immediately. This time, he decided to do the choosing. He searched the land looking for the heart after His own heart. When He finally found David, He commented, 'I've searched the land and found this David, son of Jesse. He's a man whose heart beats to my heart, a man who will do what I tell him' (Acts 13:22, MSG). In this case, God replaced a hard and self-serving heart with a soft and obedient heart – a heart that beats to His own heart. A heart that beats to God's own heart does what God's heart wants.

Interestingly, in his search for Saul's replacement, God never went to predictable areas such as palaces. Instead, He went to an unfamiliar area, a pasturing area where a young shepherd was tendering his father's sheep. He spent time examining the heart of this young man. When he was satisfied, He sent Samuel to anoint him. God never compromised his criteria no matter what – He was out looking for the heart after his own heart. When Jesse presented his seven sons, Samuel took one look at Eliab and thought he was God's anointed. You see, human standards often fail to choose the right man for the right job because the heart is hopelessly deceitful, a puzzle that no man can figure out. Men's standards are often flawed because men often look at the outer appearance, pick from the past, pick from the pecking order and too often prefer age and tenure to ability. But restating his criteria, God said to Samuel, "Do not look at his appearance or at his physical stature, because I have refused him. For the Lord does not see as the man sees, for man looks at the outward appearance, but the Lord looks at the heart" (1 Samuel 16: 7, NIV). God was literally saying to Samuel, 'I am God, boy! Looks and stature do not impress me, my chief criterion is, 'I look into the heart.' Unlike man, God looks into the heart to choose men as they really are not as they pretend to be. This criterion has already eliminated many people, noble and affluent people alike. David kept vigilant watch over his heart and God was pleased with him. When he was brought before Samuel, God said to Samuel, "Arise, anoint him, for this is the one" (1 Samuel 16:12, NJKV). It is always a man who keeps his heart with all vigilance who takes over missions arrogant people failed to fulfill.

An Upright Heart: A Heart of Praise

If the heart is upright, praise will be alright

Praise is appropriate for those who are upright in heart. I have however noticed that over the past few decades, the teachings emphasising musical skills over the uprightness of heart increased exponentially in our churches. This makes the task of selecting members to join worship teams very daunting. Often pastors responsible for selecting members are caught on either side of two extremes: Whether to ignore someone's godliness and select them because of their impressive talents or seek out the godliest people available, without considering whether they have adequate musical abilities. The life of David seems to present a balance we need to consider when selecting worship team members. David was a skilful musician, yet with an upright heart. In Psalm 33:1c,3, He says, "Praise befits the upright … Sing to him a new song; play skillfully on the strings, with loud shouts." The Scriptural balance offered here is that we must choose the gifted musicians and singers with exemplary character and passion for God to serve in our worship teams. Selecting the talented without moral integrity or godly character is as disastrous as selecting the godly without musical talent. After making mistakes in this particular issue, I developed a manual clarifying selection procedure in our church. The simple pattern used in our church consists of two key steps. First, the prospective member is subjected to technical assessment in auditions. Second, if the member is technically fit, he or she is then presented to the church council for character assessment. The council normally looks for basic predetermined character traits such as honesty, faithfulness, gentleness and commitment. There are practices that would automatically disqualify prospective members. Apostle Paul mentions these practices in Galatians 5: 19, 20. This is how we strive to maintain that Scriptural balance.

I personally admire David, not only as a moral political leader but as a worship leader as well. He had an upright heart to lead Israel and to lead worship in the temple. His heart should serve as a roadmap for all the worshippers and musicians in our churches today. He always stressed the importance of letting praise flow from an upright heart. In Psalm 119:7 (ESV), he affirms that he will praise the Lord with an upright heart. The word "upright" in this text is significant. God made people "upright," all their systems oriented toward God and His will, devoted to pleasing Him, and consecrated to His purposes and pleasure. "Heart" in this verse is used as a synecdoche and stands for the inner person, the soul in all its completion. Thus, the text implies that heart (affections), mind (understanding), and conscience (will) must all be properly attuned and earnestly engaged in order for worship to rise up to God as He intends. Adam and Eve were in this state before their fall. They had an upright heart to worship the Almighty God. All the expressions of praise must flow from an upright heart. Whether we express intense emotions when we worship Him, whether we play moving music to strike at the chords of our heart, whether we offer handclap or dance sacrifices to show God how much we appreciate Him and admire His works, all these expressions must flow from an "upright heart".

Today, worship leaders or musicians with an "upright heart" are scarce. Many are those who offer up praise to God, but do not do so with an "upright heart' and their praise is meaningless before God. In my seventeen years of ministry, I have observed that many of our worship services suffer deterioration and lack of spiritual impact. This is simply because of the nature of the heart of those men, women, and young men who serve in our worship teams. I believe that if the heart is 'upright' our praise will be 'alright'. A vibrant and compelling praise that forms and expresses a Biblical worldview does not arise from the tools and methods we use to express it. Only when the hearts of God's people have been renewed and reformed will their praise and worship be as rich, full, meaningful, and edifying as they desire. My experience has taught me that praise rising from the wellspring of an "upright heart" can be deeply felt, enthusiastically expressed, and utterly life changing.

What are the underlying elements of an upright heart? As seen in his own writings, David provides helpful descriptions ascribed to his "upright" heart: Loving (Psalm, 18:1), recognition (Psalm 9:1), obedient (Psalm 119:34), and Repentant (Psalm 25:11). Therefore, in this book I explore and discuss aspects of David's upright heart under the following chapter headings: "pure heart", "obedient heart", "repentant heart", "word-filled heart", and "servant's heart". These are the characteristics of the "upright heart" needed to make our praise and worship acceptable to God. As I expand on these five aspects of the upright heart in the next pages, I pray that what had been passed on to me will inspire and encourage pastors and worship leaders to reimagine their praise and worship ministries, and in the process empower them to experience the power of 'Praising with an upright heart.'

1

A PURE HEART

Purity is an essential precondition for true praise and worship

Whoever wants to worship God must take the opportunity to do so seriously. Israel took it seriously. The first Christian church in Jerusalem took it seriously. Their seriousness was evident in their preparation. Prior to entering the temple or synagogue to worship, they confessed sins of commission or omission, known or unknown. The confession was an important aspect of their preparation to worship God. The act of confessing sins was done as a means of purification. Hence, the Psalmist asked, "Who will truly worship God?" (Psalm 15: 1-5, 24: 3). He then gives one of the fascinating answers, "Only those whose hands and hearts are pure, who do not worship idols and never lie" (Psalm 24:3-6, NLT). God calls all the impure in heart to be sanctified, but he invites only the pure in heart to worship him in his sanctuary.

1

Purity is an essential precondition for true praise and worship. The basic sense of the Hebrew word for purity in the Old Testament is probably being clean. Purity is related to guiltless, blameless, or innocent behaviour. Purity is simply an act of emptying out a soul of any feelings of guilt so a soul can be holy, qualified to meet and see the holy God in his holy place. Without holiness no one will see the Lord (Hebrews 12:14). For worship leaders, this underscores the importance of spending time in a quite private room before leading worship, clearing up their conscience of guilt feelings. Through the act of confession, worshipper's conscience becomes whiter than the snow, purer than the clearest stream. I love leading worship but I cannot afford to do it with a guilty conscience. I always do my best and strive to have a clear conscience before God and men (Acts 24:16).

Selecting the talented without moral integrity or godly character is as disastrous as selecting the godly without musical talent

In addition, worship teams must spend at least thirty to forty-five minutes together in prayer before the commencement of a church service. The team should use this prayer time to conduct what I call a 'purity check'. The purity check that involves the team should include a special time for members to confess their public sins [false steps and offenses] to each other. James encourages this practice (James 5:16). One Sunday when speaking of the power of confession in our church, I said, 'Some people are easy to forgive and let go. When they have wronged you, they confess their wrongdoings to you not to God.' Controversial as it might have sounded, if a brother who serves with you in the worship team sins against you, and he or she only confesses his or her sin to God, you would not know he has confessed this sin to God. If he comes, flashes a smile, and hugs you, you would unwaveringly call him a hypocrite. This will hurt you even more. When this happens, the team is exposed to an imminent danger of collapse. Although it is our moral duty to forgive seventy times seven (Matthew 18:21), brothers who have sinned against us should make it easy for us to forgive them. They must confess their sins to God as well as to us, then, to forgive 490 will not be a mammoth task. According to James (5:16), healing and restoration are the benefits of the act of confessing sins to one another.

When purity checks precede sound checks, a central goal of corporate worship is achieved. I have observed a widespread tendency of worship leaders who do sound checks yet undermine purity check and this kills our corporate worship services. Only if our worshippers could learn how public worship ceremonies were conducted in the Old Testament, then the intended power of corporate worship would be fully restored. Before the Israelites could engage in any cultic or ceremonial activity, God commanded that they perform a ritual purity to consecrated or sanctify themselves (Exodus 19:10, 14, Joshua 7:13, Job 1:5). Although there is no emphasis on ritual purity in the New Testament, there is still a need for moral purity. Scripture seems to suggest two critical aspects of moral purity.

First, moral purity involves innocence in matters concerning sins (2 Cor 7:1-11). Initially, Apostle Paul's admonishing letter was not well received by many members of the Corinthian church. However, Paul indicates that he was glad that his letter finally produced sorrow which ultimately goaded some church members closer to God. He says that the admonishment turned them around and got them back in the way of salvation. They came out more alive, more concerned, more sensitive, more reverent, more human, more passionate, and more responsible. Looked at it from any angle, they came out of this correction with purity of heart. They came out innocent in the matter of the sin that Paul was addressing in their church. If he were to do it again, they would not feel any sense of guilty. They were now prepared to serve with the purity of heart. This is exactly what correction would do to those who gladly receive it. But Paul was also aware that sorrow has the power to draw some people closer to God and the power to drive some people away from God. He then distinguishes between godly sorry which produces a repentance without regret leading to salvation and worldly sorrow which produces death (2 Cor 7:10). True worshippers do not allow sorrow to drive them away from God and their pastor. They strive to remain innocent in matters regarding any sin. If they realise that they are not, they allow admonishment to yield grief that drives them closer to

God. Repentance and salvation are the fruits of godly sorrow over our sins. This godly sorrow produces purity of the heart and the purity of the heart connects us with God.

Second, moral purity is a purification that involves chastity (2 Cor 11:2). On chastity, Paul strongly warns that worshippers must, "Flee from sexual immorality. Every other sin a person commits is outside the body, but the sexually immoral person sins against his own body. Or do you not know that your body is a temple of the Holy Spirit within you, whom you have from God? You are not your own, for you were bought with a price. So glorify God in your body" Sexual immorality seems to be an inescapable sin that destroys many worshippers. As a bird is entangled in a wire net, an alarming number of worshippers, especially, worship leaders are caught in and battling with this sin. What makes things worse is that the majority of these worship leaders continue to lead our worship services without seeking any help.   Generally, moral purity involves our speech, lifestyle, love, and faith (1 Tim 4:2). Effective worship leaders strive to be examples in speech, lifestyle, love, and faith. In line with this, King David provides a useful summary of the basic character traits associated with the purity of the heart (Psalms 15:1-5). These character traits qualify worshippers to enter in God's sanctuary and praise and worship him. True worshippers

Your relationship with people is a litmus test of the purity of your heart.

and praise leaders are therefore those who walk straight and act

5

right, tell the truth from sincere heart, refuse to gossip, despise a vile person, honour those who fear the Lord, keep their word even

The word makes us different from the world. We are pure when we are different, when we think and live differently

when it cost them, and make an honest living and never take a bribe. I have noted several references to treatment of other persons which are given as direct proofs of relationship with God. I have heard many people ask, "How do I know I am morally pure?" My answer is always based on a moral perspective: "Examine your relationship with people". This is a simple, yet an accurate yardstick or purity gauge because God says, "If anyone boasts, 'I love God,' and goes on hating his brother or sister, thinking nothing of it, he is a liar. If he won't love the person he can see, how can he love the God he can't see?" (1 John 4:20, MSG). This emphasises that relationship not rules are at the heart of Christian ethics. Apostle John's inspired and frank conclusion is that a person who loves God loves other people. Your relationship with people is a litmus test of the purity of your heart. Looking at how you relate to other members in the church can help you judge if whether or not your heart is pure. A good relationship with people is a sign of the good relationship with God. So, how many worshippers are liars? These are those brothers and sisters in our churches who say they love whom they have not seen but hate their brothers and sisters whom they have seen. They lack a purity of heart and their worship is meaningless before God.

6

What is the inherent power of purity? In Matthew 5: 8, Jesus reveals the power of purity. In The Message translation the verse reads, "You are blessed when you get your inside world – your mind and heart – put right. Then you can see God in the outside world." Purity, that act of putting our inside world [our hearts] right, has the power to defy the law of invisibility. God is invisible. He said to Moses, "I will let my Goodness pass right in front of you ... But you may not see my face. No one can see me and live" (Exodus 33:20-23). Jesus says the pure in heart are blessed, so blessed that they can even see God. The "seeing" is spiritual and not literal. The reality of God cannot be fully captured by human senses. To see God is to see a visible manifestation of his presence, his character and fullness. To see God is to see his goodness. Hence, He said to Moses that He would let his goodness to pass before him. Whenever our hearts are pure, God will let his goodness pass before us. God's goodness is his observable blessings that are sometimes material and always spiritual, which ultimately generates more praises. I believe that true worshippers are spiritually and materially blessed people.

There were times when people have seen God by seeing the concrete

A 'Pure' God cannot appear to 'impure' people and a 'holy' God cannot be present with 'unholy' people

expressions of his features. For example, at Mount Sinai, God's manifestation came in the form of a cloud to reveal his character and heart deeply (Exodus 19: 16-19). Sometimes God

7

can reveal himself in the form of a fire because he is a "consuming fire" (Hebrews 12:29). It is important to note that before God manifested himself through these forms, He instructed his people to purify themselves. At Mount Sinai, before the cloud appeared the people had to obey the instruction to purify themselves. This instruction was communicating an important simple message: "A 'Pure' God cannot appear to 'impure' people and a 'holy' God cannot be present with 'unholy' people". People have to purify themselves before God's presence can appear. Likewise, when the people of Israel purified themselves, thunder and lightning, the thick cloud, the loud trumpet and the earthquake shook Mount Sinai (Exodus 19:16-19). This marks the power of purity. This is what we need in our services – thunder and lightning and earthquake.

When Isaiah encountered God in the House of praise, "The foundations trembled at the sound of the angel voices, and then the whole house filled with smoke,..." (Isaiah 6:4). I am longing for this experience when the great choruses we sing during church meetings send foundations into trembling. When this happens, sinners are bound to run to the alter exclaiming: "It's Doomsday! I'm as good as dead! Every word I've ever spoken is tainted - blasphemous even! And the people I live with talk the same way, using words that corrupt and desecrate" (Isaiah 6:5, TMS). A great song of praise sung from a pure heart will make our spiritual eyes see the King, the Lord of hosts. Because God is morally pure and by nature distinct, even with pure hearts, we suddenly become deeply aware that we are different from him. When we recognise how holy our God is, we realise how sinful we are, and in need of forgiveness. We recognise our weaknesses, mistakes, and failures.

Although due to our frailty, we cannot see the full majestic presence of God, like Moses, we can witness his passing presence in our services. The presence and actions of God will be affirmed in our lives, that we can confidently indicate that we saw God. When this happens, we will move from knowledge of God learned by tradition to the knowledge of God learned by personal experience. Therefore, being pure at the very core of our being is an awesome task. It serves as a doorway to meet, experience and to see God in our fellowship with him through the act of praise and worship.

The purity of heart comes from the word of God (John 17:17). The word of God, both spoken and written is the only chief instrument through which God purifies us. Every time he sends his Word, he does so to separate us from worldliness and equip us for service. The word makes us different from the world. We are pure when we are different, when we think and live differently. Worshippers and worship leaders and musicians can cleanse all the impurities in their hearts by becoming life-long students of the Scripture. Worshippers and Worship leaders who want to overcome any kind of sin in their lives must learn to memorise and obey God's word. A faithful study of

God's Word not only purifies the worshipper but also leads a worshipper to praise and lead others to praise effectively. Worship leaders must seek to know their Bibles better than their instruments. A percussionist must seek to know the Scripture better than the percussion. A pianist must strive to know God's word more than the piano. In this way, they will be able to lead the church into singing the word, praising the word, and praying the word. Good worship leaders passionately compose songs rich in verses from the word of God and use these songs to purify their churches through and through.

2

A WORD-FILLED HEART

A Scripture drenched heart praises well

Where shall we turn to if the methods and expressions of praise and worship have little power to rekindle our worship services and renew our members' hearts? What shall pastors and worship leaders consult if worship services become lukewarm? The sweet psalmist points in the direction of an answer: "I will praise you with an upright heart, when I learn your righteous rules" (1 Psalm 119:7, ESV). Clearly, learning God's righteous rules is the only way pastors and worship leaders can relight their worship services whenever they lapse into a state of being neither hot nor cold. It is impossible to attain a vibrant service that renews the heart, mind, and conscience without fully restoring the ministry of the word. The hearts of those who lead worship must be drenched in the word before they can dream of realising a worship service that is life changing.

Worship leaders must seek to know their Bibles better than their instruments. A percussionist must seek to know the Scripture better than the percussion

In his longest and personal Psalm 119, King David asserts that a worshipper's heart becomes upright when he or she learns the righteous rules of the Lord through study and meditation. As a worshipper himself, David highlighted the importance of Scripture by devoting 176 verses to the love of God's word. In every verse of Psalm 119, there is a synonym for the Scripture. It speaks of 'the law of the Lord', 'the commands of the Lord', 'the precepts of the Lord', 'the decrees of the Lord', or 'the statutes of the Lord'. Interestingly, we find in this psalm the same functions of the Scripture as in 2 Timothy 3:16. Generally, God's word puts us together and shapes us, so we are complete and proficient in our worship. The written word of God leads us to worship God with the uprightness of heart. In both Psalm 119 and 2 Timothy 3:16, the Holy Scripture is presented as a divine instrument that makes us live morally pure lives. It makes us angry at sin, evaluate our lives before we praise and worship, confess our sins, become examples for others and gain self-confidence as we praise.

Furthermore, Psalm 119 magnifies typical features of God's Word similar to those found in Hebrews 4:12. Looking closely at Hebrews 4:12, we notice several characteristics of God's Word:

THE WORD IS ALIVE AND PRODUCES LIFE (Hebrews 12:4a)

King David acknowledges that the word of God produces life. He prayed thus, "Turn my eyes from worthless things, and give me life through your word... Uphold me according to Your word, so I may live..." (Psalm 119:37,116ab). This means that the word restores or revives to vigorous life and health. Worshippers need to recognise that the word of God is alive. It is constantly alive. Anything that is alive is able to produce life. No matter how dead or lukewarm a worship service could be, a Scripture-saturated worshiper can bring it to life.

THE WORD IS ACTIVE AND ENERGISES

Second, the word is active (Hebrews 4:12). The word 'active' can be translated 'energes' in Greek, the word from which we get our word energy. The author of Hebrews portrays God's word as a powerful word. This makes it active, operative, energising and effective. On the other hand, David compares God's word with a light. Light is powerful and its power is unstoppable. The power of light is in its speed, so is the power of God's word. Scientifically, light is fast, even faster than sound. Light can even travel in a vacuum, such as outer space. In a vacuum, the speed of a light is 300,000,000 meters per second. Light has an incredible energy. By comparing the word of God to light, David attempt to illustrate to us that the word of

God embodies enormous energy that changes lives. The essential character of the word of God (as a light) is its inexhaustible vitality and dynamic efficacy. No matter how messed up a human life is, the word of God is capable of changing it. No matter how lifeless and unexciting a worship service is, the word of God can revitalise it.

The power of light is also in its authority over darkness. Darkness can exist only when light is absent. Light is the preeminent power. Not only is this true in the physical realm, but it is also true in the spiritual realm. Darkness (death) overshadows the heart of humankind because God's light is absent due to the fall. But, God has provided a way to deal with the power of darkness by sending His light once again. Jesus is an incarnated word and John calls this word the 'light' (John 1:5). When addressing the crowd, Jesus, himself said, "I am the light of the world. Whoever follows me will never walk in darkness, but will have the light of life" (John 8:12). Where light encounters darkness within an individual, group, or society, it is part of its innate capacity and function to overcome it. The freeing function of light is a powerful force for good. When light encounters darkness, it attracts the darkness to itself, moving it out of its place of residence.

There will be times when symptoms of darkness manifest in our church services such as doubt, fear and depression. Sometimes the devil installs counter-ideas in people's minds about reality in order to create mistrust and disbelief concerning the goodness of God and his purpose. These elements affect emotion, thought, motivation and the capacity to sense the reality of the spiritual worlds, including the reality of God. When this happens, it is the responsibility of a word-filled worship leader or pastor to illuminate the service with God's word, to throw a beam of light on the darkest areas of the service. A worship leader must speak the word to this situation. In the same way that God uses his word to heal his people and rescue them from the grave (Psalm 107:20), a Scripture saturated worship leader can use God's word to heal the church. Although a worship leader is not a preacher, he or she must discern the presence of darkness and innovatively quote or sing psalms or hymns that can bring back life and light in the worship service.

In December 2015, I was invited to lead praise and worship in one of the weddings in our area. Before calling me up to the podium to lead the church in worship, Pastor Lodwick Ramathoka said, "The man of God I am about to call had always blessed me when he renders this item. His creative stream never dries, he always find innovative ways to bless us". The comments were humbling. But in less than a minute, I dropped into a contemplative mode. Like a blazing inferno, questions sped through my mind. One of those questions was, "Exactly how do I bless these people? I asked myself quietly. Suddenly, the answer dropped into my mind as if it was an angelic whisper. 'What blesses people is not your voice but it is rather your character accompanied by a skill of applying Scripture to songs you sing'. I think this is true because my voice is not one of the finest and powerful voices. But I find innovation to bless people from the Scripture. The Scripture keeps me from just being a feel-good, fashionable, song-based kind of a worship leader. I make sure that every song I pick has Scriptural backing. In short, I am just a Scripture saturated worship leader who happens to sing some songs. Paul says, "Let the [spoken] word of Christ have its home within you [dwelling in your heart and mind] – permeating every aspect of your being] as you teach ... singing psalms and hymns and spiritual songs with thankfulness in your hearts" (Col 3:16, AMP). A person full of God's words is able to inspire others to love their Bible. His exhortations in between songs are drenched in Scripture.

Worship leaders whose hearts are void of the word of God are easy to identify. They always rely on their talents. Talent, unfortunately, is not always enough in leading worship. Talent is likely to fall short of igniting passion worship in the church. Those who depend confidently on their talents often get frustrated when their talents fail to create spark in the service.

The word of God is a divine scalpel that goes through to address any spiritual problem

Back in 2015, I attended an Easter conference in our area. There was a team of four worshippers on the stage leading songs. At the beginning, the service was lively and everybody was involved in worship. This was an enjoyable experience. Then another song leader took over and completely spoiled the experience. You know what they say, "You spoil the dish by adding too much salt." He started dancing across the floor, shouting 'Come on church stand on your feet', 'come dance with me, 'shout for the Lord', clap your hands' and 'sing louder'. He was desperate to outsmart other song leaders in the team. A majority of people, including myself, was worn out after trying hard to keep up and stopped responding. When the people sat down, he got so frustrated and began to make obnoxious comments. The service died and I could see that he had no idea of how to rekindle it. Only the Scripture would have saved the situation but he was clueless. After the service, I could see embarrassment written all over his face. Since then he never attended our fellowships. The golden rule is that do not push people to praise or worship, rather influence them to do so. Then, their response will be spontaneous. The proven approach is to get an innovative way to link the lyrics of your song with the Scripture. The Holy Spirit has always helped me in this area. A majority of God's people love Scripture, they get inspiration to stand, shout and clap from the Scripture. So, use what they love to inspire them to praise. I, therefore, urge worship leaders to learn how to sing hymns and psalms. Some of the Psalms explicitly encourage shouting, so let the church shout them.

THE WORD PIERCES AND JUDGES THE HEART

In Hebrews 4: 12, God's word is said to have an incisive and penetrating quality. It cuts its way into the innermost recesses, where no surgeon's scalpel can go. The word of God goes through the soul, the attitudes, and motives. No surgeon can correct a bad attitude, a closed mind, a rebellious spirit, a lustful heart, hypocrisy, greed, hatred, or an unforgiving spirit. These are spiritual problems and must be dealt with by spiritual means. The word of God is a divine scalpel that goes through to address any spiritual problem. The word not only pierces the heart, but it also "judges the thoughts and intentions of the heart." Likewise, David recognises that the word as "righteous judgments" decides against and punishes particular lines of thoughts and conduct (Psalm 119:7, TAB). The word "judges" means it "divides" or "separates". It analyses the evidence from our hearts. As an electronic stethoscope examines and evaluate patients' physical heart sounds, God's word penetrates into the depths of a person's spiritual being, sifting, analysing, and judging the intentions of the heart. It deals with the realm of our thinking.

David thus exclaimed, "O Lord, You have searched me and known me. You know when I sit down and when I rise up; You understand my thought from afar. You scrutinize my path and my lying down, And are intimately acquainted with all my ways" (Psalm 139:1-3). Our habit as worshippers and worship leaders must be that before we engage in worship, we surrender our hearts to God, to search them through his word. Commitment to leading a worship service should be a commitment to leading holy lifestyle. So before leading any worship service, worship leaders need to expose their hearts to God's word so their secret sins are uncovered and laid bare before God's eyes. God's word is a divine search device. As David, a praise and worship leader of old cried out, "Search me, O God, and know my heart, test me and know my anxious thoughts" (Psalm 139:23, 24, NLT), we must cry out to God to point out anything in us that offends him before we lead worship. A Scripture drenched heart praises well because it is purified from every contaminant that offends God. And a worship leader is then presented blameless before God and the church.

3

AN OBEDIENT HEART

Obedience is better than sacrifice. Submission is better than offering the fat

of rams (1 Samuel 15:22)

Since the beginning of time, obedience had always been a supreme test of fitness to lead. This is a test that a great number of leaders failed to pass. Adam was the first to fail the test. Saul's fitness to lead God's people was also tested through obedience. The test he also failed miserably. God commanded him to destroy the Amalekites under a holy ban, and everything they owned, no one and nothing was to be spared. The Lord could not have been more specific about this mission. But Saul disobeyed God by sparing Agag, king of the Amalekites and brazenly grabbed the Amalekite loot. When Samuel confronted him about his disobedience, he offered lame excuses. But Samuel was disinterested and said to him, "What is more pleasing to the LORD: your burnt offerings and sacrifices or your obedience to his voice? Listen! Obedience is better than sacrifice, and submission is better than offering the fat of rams (1 Samuel 15:22, NLT).

Obedience to God is an indispensable part of true worship. Any apparent worship service that is not accompanied by the obedience of those who render it is worthless to the individual and an insult to God. It is nothing more than rebellion and arrogance. Unlike Saul, David had developed an obedient heart since he was anointed as a king. He enjoyed a clear sense of dependence on God and made sure he fully obeyed his commandments. His obedient heart is reflected in Psalm 119: 1-8 (NLT).

In both the Old and New Testaments, the general concept of obedience relates to hearing or hearkening to a higher authority. One of the Greek terms for obedience conveys the idea of positioning oneself under someone by submitting to his or her authority and command. Another Greek word for obey in the New Testament means "to trust." Accordingly, the *Holman's Illustrated Bible Dictionary* succinctly defines biblical obedience as "to hear God's Word and act accordingly." Therefore, biblical obedience simply means, to hear, trust, submit and surrender to God and obey his Word. Therefore, a Mathematical equation for obedience can be generated as follows:

For obedience to be consummate, all four elements must be involved. Obedience starts with love. Jesus said, "If you [really] love Me, you will keep and obey My commandments" (John 14:15 AMP). Out of love comes trust. Trust begets submission. If you trust what God is saying to you, you will position yourself under the authority of his command. This is called sub-mission.

Out of love comes trust. Trust begets submission. If you trust what God is saying to you, you then position yourself under the authority of his command

If you learn to trust God, God will trust you with greater assignments and missions. However, submission without action is incomplete. Submission must lead to action. Remember, "... blessed are all who hear the word of God and put it into practice." (Luke 11:28, NLT). James adds, "But don't just listen to God's word. You must do what it says... But if you look carefully into the perfect law that sets you free, and if you do what it says and don't forget what you heard, then God will bless you for doing it (James 1:22-25, NLT). God will bless you for acting according to His word, not for just hearing it. It is when the Word of God is received with love that can stimulate trust inside you, and then an act of submitting is generated.

When arrogance and rebellion enter a man's heart, a man acts imprudently and speaks unwisely

GOD REWARDS OBEDIENCE

The rewards of obedience are fully documented in the Bible. Repeatedly we read in the Bible that God blesses and rewards obedience. Abraham's obedience was rewarded, *"And through your descendants all the nations of the earth will be blessed—all because you have obeyed me."* (Genesis 22:18, NLT). Similarly, God promised to choose from the whole earth the people of Israel and reward them with a special title, "kingdom of priests" if they listen obediently to what he says and act according to the regulations of the covenant (Exodus 19:5). Peculiar titles and blessings are the end-products of obedience not ordination." Abraham's obedience earned him a name or title 'Father of the nation'. Jacob's obedience earned him a name 'Israel'.

"Peculiar titles and blessings are resulting from obedience not ordination"

Although ordination is a Scriptural and theological act, people today tend to abuse it. They use this holy service to force 'titles' like bishops and apostles upon themselves. They do this either to gain popularity and superiority over others or as a marketing strategy to promote their ministries. In one of our preachers' meetings, I warned preachers about the rise of what I term 'title-seeking big shots.' These men and women of God are so stuck on titles that they even use the five-fold ministries as their titles. Some of these men and women get offended if you do not call them bishops, prophets or apostles. I personally

23

Ministry is not about titles but it is about missions.

believe that the words 'prophet' and 'apostle' or 'bishop' describe a duty of a person rather than a title. Some people call themselves 'bishops' without considering or meeting the strict requirements for bishops outlined by Apostle Paul (Titus 1:5-9). Worst of all is that some are not even ordained into these offices. Ministry is not about titles but it is about missions. One day while walking in our town, Tzaneen, I saw a conference advertisement that made me wince. Under one of the featured speakers' photograph was a name and titles "Bishop, Apostle, High Priest Z." I was fine when the speaker called herself bishop and apostle, but I found it to be blasphemous for any man to claim the title "High Priest" for himself. It belongs only to Jesus. Thus, when I saw this advertisement, my spirit suddenly melted within me. This time God's servant has stepped out of line and she was blinded by arrogance and the pursuit of popularity to see that. She might have the biblical right to use titles like bishops, apostles or prophets, but elevating herself to a status ascribed only to Jesus is a blatant sin. I personally believe that obedience to and fulfillment of a God-given mission is greatly satisfying than ascribed names and titles. I would rather be called brother Liphy and fulfill my God-given mission than be called apostle and fail in my God given assignments.

LEADERS REWARDING OBEDIENCE

The Bible is pregnant with stories in which God rewarded the obedience of his people. This is a valuable lesson that God is teaching church leaders. One great lesson I learned as a leader is that rewarding obedience will go a long way in motivating members. A worship leader or music director who had been obedient to your leadership, serving you and following your instructions consistently deserves a reward of obedience. You can praise him publicly and give him gifts or invent a title for him or her. In our church, I creatively designed a title for my associate who is also a loyal and obedient worship director. I call him "The Director of Praise Ministry' and this has proven to be a tremendous drive for him to do more with the worship team. He drives more than hundred and twenty kilometers to attend our worship practices and rehearsals fortnightly. He is highly motivated and because of this, the morale of the worship team is high and our worship services are sensational and power-packed. I persistently praise my keyboardist and percussionist before the church for the acts of obedience. These two young men never missed a single Sunday worship service over the past four years.

THE RIDICULOUSNESS OF SUBMISSION

Not so long ago, the Holy Spirit led me to preach under the title, "The ridiculousness of obedience and submission" in our church. The message came as I was reading the story of Hagar and Sarah (Genesis 16:1-10). This story of a maid and her mistress taught me the ridiculousness of obedience and submission. When the angel of the Lord found Hagar near the spring in the desert, he gave her a 'ridiculous' instruction, "Go back to your mistress and submit to her" (Genesis 16:9b). She was fleeing from the presence of her mistress Sarah for heaven sake! Why instruct her to return to a woman who treated her harshly? God was about to multiply her descendants exceedingly, but she first needed to pass a test of obedience or submission. When Hagar changed her attitude, the angel immediately broke the good news for her. He gave her the Sonar results, "Behold, you are with child, And you shall bear a son. You shall call his name Ishmael, Because the Lord has heard your affliction." She was so excited that she gave this God the name we sing about in our services, El Roi "God who sees". He saw what was in the seclusion of her womb. But it had to start with a ridiculous instruction which she willingly obeyed. Everything starts with our attitude to submit. Prosperity comes when we learn to submit. And submission is a voluntary attitude of giving in, of cooperating, of assuming responsibility, and of sharing a burden. Literally, the angel of the Lord was saying to her, 'Return to your mistress and cooperate with her and share her burden of bareness. You are pregnant with a child but go back and sympathise with your barren mistress.' God sees us and He is willing to give us the breakthroughs we have always wanted. But majority of us have delayed our breakthroughs because we keep failing the test of obedience and submission.

Ridiculous as it might have sounded to submit under a woman who constantly mistreated her, Hagar willingly obeyed God's instruction to go back and submit under Sarah. I know some of your can identify with Hagar's problem. One day I was reading an article portraying South African government in a bad light, showing how corrupt the president and government officials arc. I had a fccling that submitting under the government that is as corrupt as ours is as ridiculous as submitting under an abusive spouse. I know many feel the same way. But we are instructed to be in subjection to the governing authorities for there is no authority except from God (Romans 13:1-7).

Do you sometimes feel that it is ridiculous to submit under a senior pastor who is unreasonably unfair to you? Do you think it is ridiculous to submit under a leader who is less qualified than you are, who knows less than you do, a leader you are better affluent than he is? You may think so, but God demands it. David gave it to Saul, a demon possessed leader: "Whatever Saul gave David to do, he did it – and did it well" (1

Samuel 18:5, MSG). David did it so well that Saul put him in charge of his military operations. There are benefits which always accompany submission. David enjoyed them. Prosperity, wisdom and reputation are mentioned in 1 Samuel 18:5 as the benefits of obedience. People who prosper in life and gain wisdom obey God's instructions at all cost. Worshippers who succeed in life obeys their pastors.

The story of Saul and the Amalekites also teaches us the ridiculousness of obedience. Speaking through Prophet Samuel, God instructed Saul to destroy the Amalekites and everything they owned, no one and nothing was to be spared. This was a supreme test of obedience for Saul. What did he do? He and his army routed the people of Amalek, but he spared Agag, king of the Amalekites, and took for himself the best of their livestock. Why did he spare Agag? Why did he spare the best of the sheep and the oxen? It made sense to him. It was ridiculous to him to wipe away everything. When God instructed him, he might have protested in his heart, "You must be joking, God! You need the best sheep and oxen for sacrifice, don't you?" His lame excuse when Samuel confronted him about his disobedience was that he intended to sacrifice the livestock to the Lord. The rationalisation of his action was not valid because the Bible says that he went to Carmel and set monument for himself (1 Samuel 15:12). It is obvious that Saul did everything for his own glory – He set a victory monument for himself. Leaders find the instructions of the Lord ridiculous when those instructions take away the opportunity for them to be celebrated. It is only a matter of time before a leader's heart reveals its true nature, obedient towards the Lord or self-serving. When a leader's heart grows to become self-serving, every instruction which take away opportunity for him to be glorified in the eyes of people is ridiculous. Pastors should be careful. When your worship leader develops an attitude that says, "You must decrease and I increase" nothing you say to him will make sense. True and godly worship leaders commit themselves to obeying their pastors' instructions whether they fully understand those instructions or not. What they do know is "Obedience is better than sacrifices". It is ridiculous to obey instruction you do not fully understand. But there are benefits of doing so. Even if in human understanding, the instructions from the Lord seem senseless and naïve, you are still expected to submit to them.

I gave advice to so many disgruntled young pastors who decided to cut ties with their local churches. I always advice them that they should never run away from submission, instead they must learn to sort out their problems with their senior pastors or church boards. If you will not submit here, you will not submit there. If you will not submit in church A you won't submit in church B. When a new member comes to join our church, I ordinarily conduct a background check. Either this is done through one-on-one interview or through interviewing reliable sources from the

"For, if you will not submit here you will not submit there. If you will not submit in church A you won't submit in church B"

church he or she is coming from. Once I identify elements of lack of submission in his or her departure story, I immediately see a 'wandering' member. This kind does not last in the new church. I had a brother who claimed to have seen a vision in which God instructed him to join our church. But my background check on him revealed that the brother struggled with a sin of adultery, and refused to repent when the church disciplined him. Immediately, I knew that if he does not deal with this sin, he would not last in our church either. Guess what! The same thing that made him leave his previous church made him leave our church. He refused to be disciplined again. In all likelihood, if a person fails to submit in Church A, he or she will fail to submit in Church B. How so? Submission says more about a person's attitude than about the person under whom a person is expected to submit or a place where submission is expected to take place.

Pastors must learn to identify early signs of disobedience in the life of their worship leaders and members of the worship team. The first time Saul failed the test of obedience was when Samuel failed to show up at Gilgal (1Samuel 13). On this occasion Samuel is late arriving (delayed) at the battlefield, Saul conducts the sacrifice himself. One prime test of obedience is the "test of delay". What does your worship leader do when you are delayed? Does he step out of line and hijack your pastoral role? Does he, instead, of introducing a song start preaching or does he do things he would not do when you are present? What your worship leader and worship team members do when you arrive late to the meeting or service or crusade demonstrates their obedience or a lack thereof.

In this occasion when Samuel delayed for seven days, Saul hijacked his priestly role. Only priests were allowed to offer sacrifices, but Saul took things into his own hands and sacrificed burnt and peace offerings. By usurping the priestly role, Saul showed an astonishing lack of discernment. Saul had been anointed king, but kingly anointing was not priestly anointing. Likewise, a worship leading anointing is not a pastoral anointing. Samuel had explained the "regulations of the kingship" (1 Samuel 10:25), but Saul trespassed on them. When people intentionally step out of their God-ordained roles, they leave a disgraceful legacy. God sent Samuel to tell Saul that because of his conduct and arrogant action, his kingdom is about to be handed to someone else. A man's disobedience invites God's rejection. Disobedience is the beginning of the end for any leadership under the sun. Samuel said to Saul, "... Because you have rejected the word of the Lord, he has rejected you as king" (1 Samuel 15: 23cd, NIV).

SUBMITTING TO THE AUTHORITY OF LEADERS

Over and above obeying God, believers are urged to obey their leaders. Why should believers obey their church leaders? Hebrews 13:17 provides three fundamental reasons. First, leaders watch out for their souls and guard their spiritual welfare. Second, leaders must give account to God. Finally, so they [leaders] do the work of ministry without sighing and groaning for that would not profit them. Therefore, believers must be responsive to their pastoral leaders, listening to their instructions. As stewards, they work under strict supervision of the Almighty God. When their life ends, they will answer for how responsibly they tended to His divine vision and values. Christians must do their part to contribute to the joy of their leadership, not its drudgery. Any congregation that makes things harder for its leaders, disadvantages itself. To benefit from a ministry of your pastor, you need to respect and follow him or her heartily and avoid hurting him or her. Sometimes *A man's disobedience invites God's rejection.* ago I came across a principle which says, "Hurting people hurt others and are easily hurt by them." Although this is highly discouraged, it would seem so natural for a hurting pastor to hurt his members. It is the most difficult thing to preach while licking wounds caused by men and women under your care. Although the Holy Spirit always helps us to restrain our emotions, it is natural that the sermons would have

32

corrective and confrontational elements here and there. And this cannot benefit the congregation.

4

A REPENTANT HEART

"Unrepentant people turn to crucify those who correct them"

It is in the nature of arrogant men to offer excuses when confronted with their sins. Arrogant men do not own their mistakes and sins. They instead look for ways to gloss over them. Like all arrogant political leaders before him, when confronted with his sin, Saul could not own up to his mistakes. He had plenty of excuses for his disobedience instead. His main excuses for offering unlawful sacrifice were that Samuel delayed to show up at Gilgal and his soldiers were already panicking and slipping away (1 Samuel 13). Like Saul, many offer excuses to justify and spiritualise their actions because of their so-called "special" circumstances. We often blame our mistakes and sins on forces of circumstances. Still even after mentioning circumstances that led to sinful actions, the small voice in our conscience remains unquiet as an indication that God does not buy into our excuses. This voice can only be silenced by repentance. God forgives, restores, and blesses only when we

God forgives, restores, and blesses only when we are honest about our mistakes and sins

are honest about our mistakes and sins.

God expects leaders to seek and obey his will at all cost despite their circumstances, and if they do not, they leave him no choice but to replace them. Likewise, Saul was replaced with King David, a man after his own heart. Unlike Saul, David though not perfect, though not immune from failure, he had a repentant heart. A repentant heart is a heart of praise, a heart after God's own heart. One popular incident in David's life offers us a lesson about repentance as a worship leader (2 Sam 11:1-5). One evening, he got up from his bed and strolled on the roof of the palace. From his vantage point on the roof, he saw a woman bathing, and lust filled his heart. He should have left the roof and fled the temptation. Instead, he went further by enquiring about Bathsheba. And because the woman was stunningly beautiful, David sent his agents to get her. After she arrived, he went to bed with her. Then she returned home. But before long she realised she was pregnant.

In the morning, David wrote a letter to Joab and sent it with Uriah. In that letter he wrote, "Put Uriah in the front lines where the fighting is the fiercest. And pull back and leave him exposed so that he is sure to be killed". So Joab, holding the city under siege, put Uriah in a place where he knew there were valiant men. When the city's defenders came out to fight Joab, some of David's soldiers were killed, including Uriah. How could a man remembered and respected as an outstanding worship leader whose reputation and skills earned him a place as a harpist in the king's palace act cruelly? How could a man after God's own heart do what King David did to Uriah?

This story illustrates the power of lust. Like many worship leaders today, David allowed lust to stay in his heart and allowed it to entice and drag him away from God. His transgression represents a classic example of the growth of sin mentioned by James, "But every man is tempted, when he is drawn away of his own lust, and enticed. Then when the lust hath conceived, it bringeth forth sin, and sin, when it is finished, bringeth forth death" (Jas 1: 14, 15). Temptation comes from evil desires inside us, not from God. It begins with an evil thought and becomes sin when we dwell on the thought and allow it to become an action. Like a snowball rolling downhill, sin's destruction grows the more we let sin have its way. Someone once said, "The best time to stop snowball is at the top of the hill, before it is too big or moving too fast to control." Trustworthy worshippers are those who are able to abort lust before it gives birth to sin. Failure to abort lust at conception has devastating consequences. David learned this the hard way. God was at all not pleased with his action and brought his disciplining intervention.

However, when Nathan, boldly rebuked him, David replied, "I have sinned against the Lord". Instead of hiding behind excuses like Saul, David acknowledged his sin before God. God pardoned him of his blasphemous

Jesus has a laundry service and he wants us to present our dirty hearts for washing. His blood washes whiter than snow

behaviour. The story of Saul and David teaches us that we will always have two types of men in the world, men of 'excuses' and men of 'sorries'. A man of 'sorry' believes that willingness to admit mistakes is the first step in dealing with them. Whilst a man of 'excuses' believes that saying sorry is the sign of weakness. The weakness of many powerful and influential praise leaders is not their failure to resist the sin of sexual immorality, but it is rather their failure to acknowledge it. One big lesson the life of David teaches us is that while he sinned greatly, he did not sin repeatedly. Unlike many worship leaders today, David did not make one mistake over and over again.

Reading the story of David and Bathsheba today, we can easily see why sexual immorality is predominantly the main hindrance of worship in the church. Many influential and powerful leaders,

We will always have two types of men in the world, men of 'excuses' and men of 'sorries'

whether they are pastors or worship leaders, just find this sin to be irresistible. No matter how intimate with God we may be, not one of us is immune to sin. However, God is quick to respond with forgiveness when we confess our sins knowing that "He who covers his sins will not prosper" (Proverbs 28:13). David teaches us that we should never take God's forgiveness lightly or his abundant grace for granted. David experienced the overwhelming joy of forgiveness even when he had to suffer the consequences of his sins. He always lived with great energy and joy because of God's forgiveness. Forgiveness produces peace and joy in our spirits. When we sin, our sin produces a sense of guilt that should make us turn to God humbly with broken heart asking for forgiveness.

Sin is terrible, but God's mercy is greater than our guilt. The proper function of guilt is not to make us hide as Adam did, but it is to lead us to take full responsibility for our sins and acknowledge them, confess them and renounce them. When we do this, God will bring us out of the gray exile of sin and rebellion into a marvelous light and the joy of God's salvation will start to fill our hearts and lead us to sing anthems of praise to the Lord. God' salvation turns our mourning into dancing again, put off our sackcloth, and clothed us with gladness that our hearts may sing to the Lord and not be silent (Ps 30:11, 12). David was indeed a "man after God's heart", a worshipper who stands as a true model we should follow in order to preserve the power and the anointing of praise and worship.

Repentance opens a door for God to create in us a pure heart. David says in one of his penitent psalms, "Create in me a pure heart, O God... Do not cast me from your presence or take your Holy Spirit from me. Restore to me the joy of your salvation and grant me a willing spirit, to sustain me ...O Lord, open my lips and my mouth will declare your praise.... The sacrifices of God are a broken spirit, a broken and contrite heart" (Ps 51: 10, 15, 17). The word "create" is a Hebrew "bara" which means to form out of nothing. This is God's unique action. The gravity of David' sin made him feel that for God to remove the curse of this terrible wrongdoing from his conscience would take a miracle comparable to the miracle of bringing the world into existence from nothing. He was longing for a spiritual miracle which is far more astonishing compared to those concerned with tangible world. David believed as deeply as he could that God was loving and forgiving. And God filled a void caused by sin in his heart as he did in the creation of the universe. The hovering Spirit returned into his heart and regenerated him.

David's personal penitence in the Old Testament is unparalleled even in New Testament dispensation. In his poignant plea for God's pardon, he asked God to soak and scrub him in his laundry. Jesus has a laundry service, and he wants us to present our dirty hearts for washing. His blood washes whiter than snow. The "sorry" attitude will certainly preserve the power of praise in our churches. The world we live in poses a serious challenge to us, but we need the kind of heart the Psalmist possessed. The heart that is penitent and repentant, not the heart that gives God excuses.

My experience with unrepentant people

Working with unrepentant people is like working with the old time Pharisees. If someone tries to rebuke them, they get angry and offended. They refuse to have a heart receptive to rebuke. This is one of the valuable lessons my experience in working with the church has taught me. I remember that I once had a powerful worship leader, with an amazing voice and voice control. She was absolutely the best worship leader I ever had. When she became pregnant, it was a bolt from the blue. I felt let down. I felt even more disappointed after learning that it was a young man I loved dearly who impregnated her. They were both in the worship team. What hurt me the most was that when I rebuked both of them publicly and suspended them from all the church activities, they became bitter, a feeling they harboured for months.

Every once in a while people fall into fornication and adultery, that doesn't bother me anymore. But what bothers me most is how those who have sinned react to correction. These two members became very angry at correction and finally decided to leave the church. Since they were both in the worship ministry, their departure paralysed our worship team. Thank God, the two ultimately came to their senses, repented and came back to our church. They got married and are now back with the worship team. Their earnestness and passion to serve God and the church continue to grow every day. Like the old-time Pharisees, unrepentant people think rebuke undermines their external righteousness. Unrepentant people see any rebuke as a personal attack.

A few years ago, a woman from one of the neighbouring churches joined our church. I was excited about this because I saw a potential in her from the go. But no later than seven months, all my excitement about her joining our church vanished like a morning dew. She began sending me witty and seductive text messages. The Bible says, "The lips of a seductive woman are oh so sweet, her soft words are oh so smooth. But it won't be long before she's gravel in your mouth, a pain in your gut, a wound in your heart" (Proverbs 5:3, 4). The frightening warnings in these verses awakened fears in me I didn't know I had. I knew this was a disaster waiting to happen. I then sought for the most effective ways to avert the disaster. I thought confrontation was the best way to go about

"Like the old-time Pharisees, unrepentant people think rebuke undermines their external righteousness. Unrepentant people see any rebuke as a personal attack"

resolving this issue. I then confronted and rebuked her. I asked her to stop. When she persisted, my wife confronted her, but instead of repenting, she became bitter as wormwood. She became hostile towards my wife and literally stopped talking to her. She openly defied her instructions as a leader of the women's ministry. This was a stressful time for my wife. I asked myself, "Why was she crucified when she has done nothing wrong?" I think this was exactly what happened to Jesus. When he rebuked the Pharisees, they crucified him. When he called

41

out their sins, they did not repent, instead, they nailed him to the cross. It is in the nature of the unrepentant heart to get offensive when rebuked and corrected. Unrepentant people tend to crucify those who correct them.

It is in the nature of unrepentant heart to get offensive when rebuked and corrected. Unrepentant people tend to crucify those who correct them

Likewise, when we confronted this woman and pointed out at her sins, she immediately went on the offensive. All of a sudden, she quit attending Friday worship services and deliberately arrived late for Sunday meetings. What hurt me most was the fact that she became more and more rebellious and disrespectful. Without shame, she would move outside the church every time I stood up on the pulpit to preach. She then accused me of being ruthless, condemning, and unforgiving. Well, it is not rare for people who are unwilling to repent of their sins to make a list of sins to the persons rebuking them. Their chief concern is to protect their reputation and their external righteousness.

In my distress, I sought the face of God through prayer and fasting. Experiences with rebellious and unrepentant people will make you pray harder. You will feel like praying because the experience of rebellion is very sobering. One night I had a dream that changed my entire perception of the whole situation. It was so dreadful that my mind could have rejected it had the Lord not confirmed it. The Lord showed me that the devil wanted to destroy the church by tricking me into three

42

dangerous spirits: adultery, anger and unforgiving. He only looked for an agent whose heart was not right at the time. I was so relieved to know that her arrogance, bitterness, and rebellion were issues of her heart.

To be honest, I might have easily overcome the spirit of adultery right away, but I had to struggle with the most powerful spirits of anger and unforgiving for more than three months. I think this are far more powerful spirits than the spirit of adultery. For all these months, my prayer and that of my associate pastor was that she must either repent or leave our church. Unforgiving spirit provokes hateful feelings against the traitor. My prayer is an example of a prayer that most hurting people pray often. A hurting King David prayed this prayer in Psalm 55:2-15. He prayed to God that his enemies be destroyed and taken down to hell alive. It is easy for leaders to pray that disobedient and rebellious people around them die and go to hell immediately or leave their churches. Thank God that my painful experience with unrepentant people have taught me two important lessons about forgiveness. First, forgiveness is unconditional. Second, forgiveness is a medicine for our spirits. I learned that modern time unrepentant Pharisees shall never cease to exist in our churches, but worshippers and pastors must learn to forgive them unconditionally as our heavenly Father forgave them all their transgressions and iniquities.

43

5

A SERVANT'S HEART

"Servants surrender their lives, rights, and preferences in order to satisfy, enrich and edify others"

A moral duty of any worship leader is to serve. David proved to be a classic servant since he was young. When Saul disobeyed God, the Spirit of the Lord left him and the evil spirit that filled him with depression and fear tormented him thereafter. Some of his servants suggested that he should find a good musician to play a soothing music on a harp whenever the

Everything about worship goes wrong when our worship leaders become preoccupied with status and positions rather than serving

tormenting spirit is troubling him and he shall be well again. So David was recruited to serve as a musician in the courts of King Saul. The Bible says, "So David went to Saul and began serving him. Saul loved David very much, and David became his armor bearer. Then Saul sent word to Jesse asking, "Please let David remain in my service, for I am very pleased with him"

44

(1Samuel 16:14-22). David's journey to greatness started with him serving in the courts of King Saul as a low man, a servant, a musician and an armorbearer. He did what Saul told him to do with great attitude and Saul was very pleased with him. Every senior pastor needs a worship leader with the same attitude as David's, a worshipper with a servant's heart that is committed to higher principles of servanthood. The lesson worship leaders should learn from David is that great leaders move from serving to leading. Before I became a pastor, I started off serving in crusade meetings and home cells as a song leader. I know countless others who started as worship leaders serving their pastors and their local churches and ended up being pastors leading big churches.

Our Lord Jesus taught his disciples that the greatest must be the servant. He said, "Whoever wants to be a leader among you must be your servant, and whoever wants to be first among you must become your slave." (Matthew 20:25-27). Everything about worship goes wrong when our worship leaders become preoccupied with status and positions rather than serving. Serving as a worshipper is like giving your life to others as our Lord said, "For even the Son of Man came not to be served but to serve others and to give his life as a ransom for many." Servants surrender their lives, rights and preferences in order to satisfy, enrich and edify others. Servant-minded worshippers are like ransoms for many Christians in their churches. They have to pay for their freedom by surrendering their own freedom.

SEVEN GUIDING PRINCIPLES OF A SERVANT-WORSHIPPER

King David was a principled servant-worshipper. Here I examine seven principles that guided his heart as a great servant-worship leader. These principles are unveiled in 1 Samuel 24, 26 and 2 Samuel 1-4, 9:

Principle 1: A servant's heart never takes advantage of the opportunity for vengeance

"A servant's heart never takes advantage of the opportunity for vengeance" When an opportunity for killing Saul presented itself, David refused to take it. Having suffered from Saul's violent jealousy, David exemplified an attitude of non-retaliation against his enemy. He did not take advantage of the opportunity to kill Saul even though Saul had tried to kill him many times. A servant's heart does not harbor vengeance and hatred. David's attitude towards his master teaches us that the opportunity to defeat your leader is not a permission to do so. Even when Abishai advised him that Saul should be pinned to the earth with one stroke of the spear, he resisted a temptation to do so. When Recab and Baanah thought David would be impressed that they took vengeance on the family of

Desire for vengeance has no place in the life of a servant committed to God Saul on his behalf, he grew angry and killed them. The mark of a great servanthood is the capacity to refuse usurping power when overzealous people around us demand we do so. Pastors are humans and can sometimes be tempted to be jealous of your successes, hate you; they can even go as far as attempting to assassinate you or your character. However, you need to know that vengeance and vindication are under God's control.

Servants do not kill their masters. David recognised that by manipulating his way to power would only break trust. Trust between the senior pastor and his worship leader is often broken when a worship leader looks for the opportunity to destroy his pastor when he is in his weaker state. Trust is a positive expectation that another will not through words, actions, or decisions act opportunistically. The dimensions of trust include integrity (honesty and truthfulness) and consistency (an individual's reliability, predictability). Mistrust drives out trust and trust beget trust. After David spared the life of Saul, his master, he was trusted more. A servant who is willing to spare the integrity of his master will be trusted more.

Principle 2: Commitment to God serves as the basis for commitment to those God has anointed as His servants.

The reason David did not carry out the human desire for vengeance on his master is that he was so devoted to his God. A desire for vengeance has no place in the life of a servant committed to God. Many things can disqualify someone from worship, and unrestrained vengeance is one of the most powerful ones. David was able to overcome the desire to retaliate against Saul. His honorable actions reveal his commitment to the legitimate holder of the throne, Saul, "the Lord's anointed". It is easy to submit to the authority of your master when you have first submitted yourself to the authority of God who appointed your master.

Principle 3: A servant's heart submits until the end

When Saul was tormented by the spirit. that filled him with depression and fear [A sign that he has fallen from grace], David faithfully served him as a musician who played a soothing harp. Even still, when he heard that Saul was dead he deeply wept for him. Why did he honour a man who tried to murder him in the palace and chased him through hills and caves in order to execute him? A servant's heart knows that submission has little to do with the person in charge, but it is God's command (Hebrews 13:17). When a young Amalekite told David that he stood over Saul and killed him at Saul's request,

David ordered that he be executed. He said, "Why were you not afraid to kill the Lord's anointed one?" David learned submission through submission and did so until the death of his master. A servant who submits until the end earns his or her influence and honour and receives more authority from God. Servants owe submission to their leaders until the end.

Principle 4: A servant's heart remains loyal to the master and protects his integrity at all cost

A heart of a servant is loyal and humble. Loyalty is simply the willingness to protect and save face for another person. This is exactly what David did. He even went further to protect Saul's integrity even after he was slain. He composed this lamentation song for his master: "The beauty of Israel is slain on your high place! How the mighty have fallen! Tell it not in Gath, Proclaim it not in the streets of Ashkelon – Lest the daughters of the Philistines rejoice, Lest the daughters of the uncircumcised triumph" (2 Samuel 1:19, 20). Why do we always tell it when our mighty leaders have fallen? Why do we proclaim it in the streets when our pastors have fallen and let the pagans laugh in triumph? But David's song for Saul shows that a faithful servant is willing to protect his master's integrity at all cost.

Principle 5: A servant's heart repays his master good for evil all the times

When David had finished speaking, Saul called back, "Is that really you, my son David?" Then he began to cry. And he said to David, You are a better man than I am, for you have repaid me good for evil. Yes, you have been amazingly kind to me today, for when the Lord put me, you didn't do it (1 Samuel 24:16-18). A servant is always kind to his leader despite the leader's evil intentions to destroy him. When Saul dumped evil on him, David heaped good on him. Saul thus prayed God to give David his servant a bonus of blessings for what he has done. In addition, Saul was now certain beyond reasonable doubt that God has given David, his servant, the kingdom of Israel. A kind servant will always receive kind words from his leader. Saul prophesied that God has taken Israel's kingdom from him and given it to David. Do you sometimes imagine you pastor calling you to his office saying to you that the Lord has given you 'this' church to lead? This can happen if you remain kind to your pastor no matter what. These are the benefits of respecting your leader as a servant and repaying him good for evil all the time.

Principle 6: A trustworthy servant makes and keeps promises to his master

When David spared Saul's life for the first time, Saul asked him to swear by the Lord that he will not destroy his line of descendants when he finally becomes a king. He said "And now I know indeed that you shall surely be king ... Therefore swear now to me by the Lord that you will not cut off my descendants after me, and that you will not destroy my name from my father's house." So David swore to Saul..." (1 Samuel 24:20-22). David kept this promise. Long after Saul and Jonathan's death, David remembered his promise to his master and returned a favour to his master and his friend, Jonathan. Then he said, "Is there not still someone of the house of Saul, to whom I may show the kindness of God?" And Ziba said to the king, "There is still a son of Jonathan who is lame in his feet."

David kept his promise to his master through a kindness shown to Mephibosheth, Jonathan's lame son. He restored to him all of Saul's belongings, he ordered servants to cultivate his land, and he provided food, income, and a role at the court. Indeed David never destroyed Saul's line of descendants as per promise instead he exalted a crippled Mephibosheth to eat at his table like one of the king's sons. What a servant indeed! There is only one simple rule to determine who your trustworthy servants are. Those who make and honour their promises are real servants. They honour the promises they made to their masters even after their masters are long gone.

51

Principle 7: A servant serves the master with an ultimate humility even when the master has drastically failed in his leadership role

Humility is a mark of true servanthood. Generally, all servants have humble hearts. A humble heart is a heart that is willing to stoop low and serve the leader even when the leader's leadership has stalled. David's heart of humility shamelessly exalted a humiliated master and incessantly called him, 'The anointed of the Lord' (1Samuel 24:6-10) even after the anointing was long gone. A servant who fails to humble himself/herself to serve those God has raised will eventually act out of selfish motives and hurt the church of God. A heart of a servant is capable of making ultimate sacrifices to let the team win and cannot serve its own selfish interests. Remember, God gives grace to the humble (James 4:6), but pride brings disgrace (Pr 11:2).

www.ingramcontent.com/pod-product-compliance
Lightning Source LLC
Chambersburg PA
CBHW060702030426
42337CB00017B/2721